BOYS TOWN Press

Boys Town, Nebraska

I0800577

Responsible ME!

TEACHER ACTIVITY GUIDE

Written by

Julia Cook

Illustrated by

Anita DuFalla

Responsible Me! Teacher Activity Guide

ISBN 978-1-944882-48-8

Published by Boys Town Press
13603 Flanagan Blvd., Boys Town, Nebraska 68010

Printed in the United States
10 9 8 7 6 5 4 3

For a Boys Town Press catalog, call 1-800-282-6657
or visit our website: BoysTownPress.org

BOYS TOWN. Saving Children Healing Families
Boys Town Press is the publishing division of Boys Town, a national organization serving children and families.

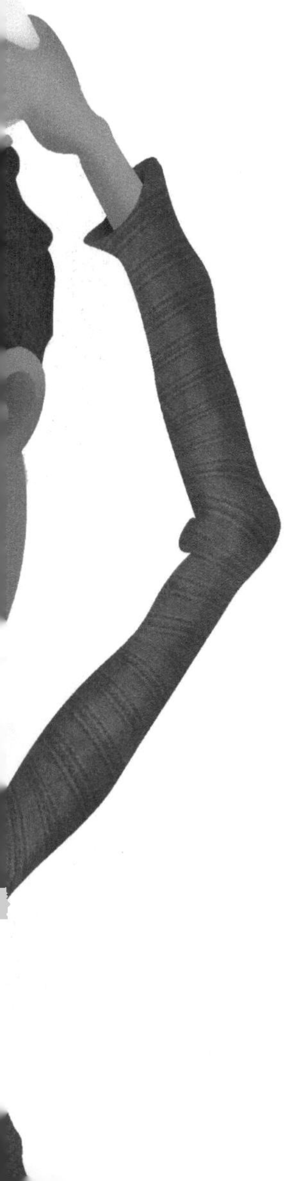

Everyone's favorite fourth-grader,

Noodle,

has learned a lot over the course of his storybooks! And it's time to share some of those lessons with your class!

Inside this guide, you'll find activities designed to teach and reinforce the life lessons from all six storybooks.

Instructions to Download Worksheets and Handouts

ACCESS:

boystownpress.org/book-downloads

ENTER:

Your first and last names
Email address
Code: 944882rmag488
Check yes to receive emails to ensure your email link is received.

Baditude! -- ACTIVITY #1

What's Bugging Me?

INTRODUCTION

Sometimes we have a Baditude and we don't see it coming. Sometimes, when Baditudes happen, it's for reasons we can control, and sometimes it's for reasons we cannot control. Becoming more aware of what is making us unhappy is key to having a more positive attitude.

Materials Needed

- *Baditude!* storybook (optional)
- "What's Bugging You?" worksheet
- Pen or pencil
- Paper strips
- Fly swatter (Ideally, one per student; however, you can use one per group if students will be taking turns.)

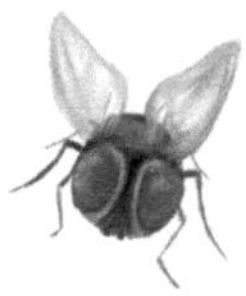

Teacher Instructions

1. (Optional) Read *Baditude!*, by Julia Cook, to the class.
2. Pass out a "What's Bugging You?" worksheet to each student.
3. Divide the class into groups of 3-4, and provide each group with one *shared* "What's Bugging You?" worksheet.
4. Allow students to have a 10-minute brainstorming session on things that bug them and why.
5. Have one person in the group write down all of the "bugs" on the shared worksheet.
6. Direct students to write down some of the things that bug them on the individual "What's Bugging You?" worksheet on the Bug side. (Students can use the group list and come up with others of their own.)
7. As a group, have students discuss which bugs are within their control and which bugs are out of their control and why.

8. Explain to students that they can use different strategies to swat away "bugs." Examples might include the following: if your "bug" is that you don't like getting up early when you're tired, you could try going to bed a bit earlier the next night to see if that helps. Have students discuss strategies for swatting away "bugs."
9. Tell students to turn their bugs over and write "Swat the Bug" at the top.
10. Each student should write down a few strategies on their "What's Bugging You?" worksheet on the Swat side.
11. Have each group share one bug with the class, along with a strategy to swat it away.
12. Have students copy their bugs onto strips of paper of various sizes.
13. Crinkle them into little balls.
14. Have students swat them away using the fly swatters as they reflect on their swatting strategies.
15. Enlist all students to clean up their bugs.

Name ______________________________

What's Bugging You?

DIRECTIONS: Write a list of things that bug you on the large bug. When finished, flip the paper over and write "Swat the Bug" at the top.

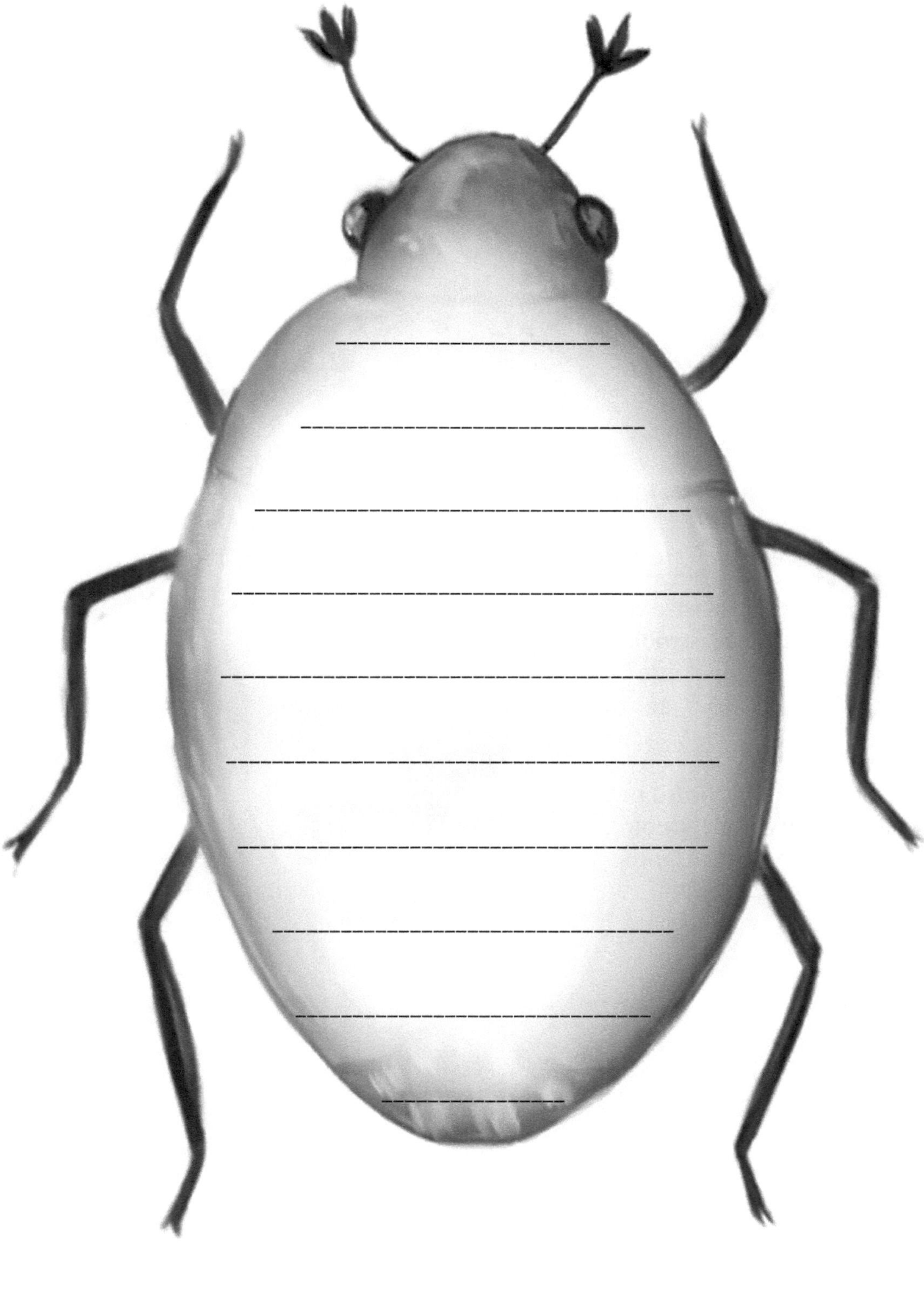

Baditude! -- ACTIVITY #2

Ping Pong Positive!!!

INTRODUCTION

Baditude is contagious. It spreads like a cold or the flu. Fortunately, a positive attitude is also contagious, but it takes a little more work. Becoming more aware of our actions and our words can really make a difference to us and those around us.

Materials Needed

- *Baditude* storybook (optional)
- Ping pong balls
- 2 identical, empty clear containers—one labeled "Ping Pong Positive" and the other labeled "Baditude."

Teacher Instructions

1. (Optional) Read *Baditude*, by Julia Cook, to the class.
2. Each time a notable positive statement or action is heard or demonstrated in the classroom, place one ping pong ball into the "Ping Pong Positive" jar.
3. Each time a negative statement or action is heard or demonstrated in the classroom, place two ping pong balls into the "Baditude" jar. Explain that negativity is twice as hard to overcome.
4. When the "Ping Pong Positive" jar is full, hold a classroom celebration, then start over.

Ideas for Classroom Celebrations

Extra recess

Popcorn party

Free assignment pass

Extra free-choice time

Baditude! -- ACTIVITY #3

Are You Sleeping? Are You Sleeping?

INTRODUCTION

Baditudes often happen because kids don't get enough sleep. Lack of sleep can lead to irritability, anxiety, and depression. Becoming more aware of how much sleep you are getting and how much sleep you actually need can really make a difference in everything you do!

Materials Needed

- "Sleep Log" worksheet – 2 per student
- Group contract
- 3 pictures of a phone battery – 1 fully charged, 1 half-charged, and 1 low
- Battery-charged handheld vacuum cleaner with one-quarter charge
- Construction paper
- Colored pencils or markers

Objectives

- Students will be more aware of how sleep affects performance.
- Students will determine how much sleep they are actually getting.
- Students will develop strategies for getting more sleep, if needed.

Teacher Instructions

1. Pass out sleep logs and have each student honestly record the amount of sleep they get each night over a seven-day period. Remind students that being truthful with themselves about their sleep habits is essential to the success of this activity.

2. After collecting sleep data for the week, have students determine whether they are getting enough uninterrupted sleep (8 to 10 hours per night).

3. Show students the phone battery images. Explain that sleep recharges both the body and the brain. To get the most out of everything they do, they need to start each day with a fully charged body and mind. When screen time takes over, we often sacrifice sleep to get everything done. The problem is, without enough rest, we run out of energy and can't do our best.

4. Turn on the vacuum cleaner and demonstrate that, at first, it has plenty of energy. But as time goes on, the battery wears down—and so does its performance. This is similar to what happens when we come to school tired because we didn't get enough sleep to recharge our battery—our brain. When the energy is gone, we're done. We can't learn, grow, or perform without it.

5. Explain that when the human brain doesn't get enough sleep, the first symptom is irritability, followed by anxiety, which can eventually lead to depression. All of these can lead to a Baditude and a much less better YOU!

6. Sort students into groups of 3-4 and have them discuss strategies that can help them get more sleep (scheduling their time better, cutting back on screen time, getting more physical exercise, eating healthier, keeping digital devices out of their bedroom, etc.).

7. Have each group complete a personalized group contract promising to implement the proposed group strategies individually for one week.

8. While implementing strategies, have students record a second sleep log.

9. At the end of week two, have students compare their sleep logs to see whether they were able to get more sleep effectively.

10. Have each student write a reflection of this activity and/or draw a before and after picture of themselves after implementing the group sleep strategies. *(Did school/life in general seem easier when you were able to get adequate sleep? How? etc.)*

Name ________________________________

Sleep Log

DIRECTIONS: Record the date and time you actually fell asleep (not the time you went to bed), the time(s) you woke up, and the total amount of sleep you got that night—listed in hours and minutes.

	Went to Sleep	Times I woke up	Woke up	Total Sleep
				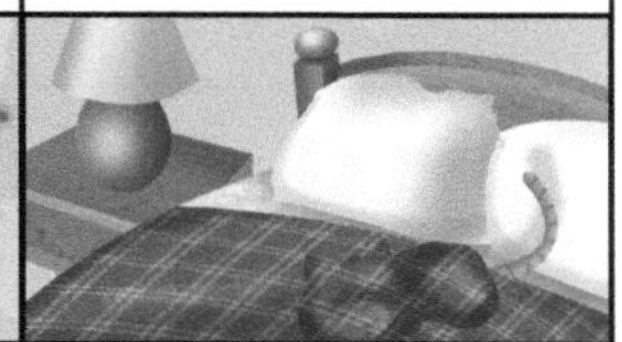
SATURDAY				
FRIDAY				
THURSDAY				
WEDNESDAY				
TUESDAY				
MONDAY				
SUNDAY				

Group Contract

As a group, we agree to implement the following strategies into our daily routines to help us get more sleep. We promise to use these strategies faithfully and honestly for one week.

____

____

____

____

____

____

____

____

____

____

____
student signature date

____
teacher signature

Baditude! -- ACTIVITY #4

The Happy Reminder Rock ☺

INTRODUCTION

Sometimes we get so caught up with all that is going on in our lives that we forget to smile. Smiling does wonderful things for you both on the inside and on the outside.

Materials Needed

- Rocks of various sizes and shapes
- Paint brushes
- Paint
- Pictures of happy/fun expressions

Teacher Instructions

1. Choose a rock that fits your personality.
2. Paint it your favorite color. Dry thoroughly.
3. Choose an expression that makes you smile and draw/paint that expression on the rock.
4. Place your rock on your desk, and whenever you see it, make a conscious effort to share your amazing smile with others.
5. Allow your smiling outside to sink into your inside.

GUESS WHAT ELSE?

You can also do this activity to make a **CHEATING PREVENTION ROCK.** It keeps you honest when you are taking tests. (*Cheaters Never Prosper!*)

Keep Your Eyes on the Prize

Baditude! -- ACTIVITY #5

Balcony Attitudes and Basement Attitudes (Baditude vs Gratitude)

INTRODUCTION

There are two types of attitudes that define people in the world... **balcony attitudes** and **basement attitudes**. People with balcony attitudes view the world through positive, hopeful, optimistic eyes. These people tend to attract others and usually have lots of friends. People with **basement attitudes** see only the negative and tend to be pessimistic by nature. This can make it harder to connect with others. Which are you?

Materials Needed

- *Baditude!* storybook (optional)
- "Basement Attitudes/Balcony Attitudes" worksheet
- "Basement vs Balcony" worksheet
- Paper and pencil

Objectives

- Students will develop a better understanding of attitude and how one's attitude might affect others.
- Students will understand that attitude is a choice – both positive and Baditude!

Teacher Instructions

1. (Optional) Read *Baditude!*, by Julia Cook, to the class.
2. Pass out a "Basement Attitudes/Balcony Attitudes" worksheet to the class.
3. Instruct students:
   * Brainstorm a list of 20-25 people that you know. Try to pick people from all aspects of your life – home, family, friends, teams, activities, etc.
   * Ask yourself, "Is this person full of gratitude most of the time, or does this person have Baditude?" Then list them under the appropriate heading on the worksheet.
   * Next to each name, jot down a short reason for why you put them in that column. For example: John – (balcony) because he always smiles; Jake – (basement) because he complains about math class every day.
4. Pass out a "Basement vs Balcony" worksheet to students.
5. Have students complete the worksheet based on their list.
6. Discuss students' answers. Explain that most people don't have balcony attitudes EVERY day – we all have bad days. But there are things we can do to have a balcony attitude more often than a basement attitude. Discuss those strategies as a class.

 Name ______________________

Basement vs Balcony

DIRECTIONS: Answer the questions below.

1. Look at your list and think about who you would rather be around: Your friends with basement attitudes or your friends with balcony attitudes. Why? ______________________

____

____

2. Looking at your basement list, try to figure out why that person might be in the basement, and think of what he or she needs to get to the balcony. ______________________

____

____

3. Is there anything that you can do to help that person? ______________________

____

____

4. What about you? Are you in the basement or the balcony? Why? ______________________

____

____

5. What things can you do to move to the balcony if you are in the basement? ______________________

____

____

6. What things can you do to stay in the balcony for a very long time? ______________________

____

____

Basement Attitudes/Balcony Attitudes

DIRECTIONS: Make a list of 20-25 people you know. Try to pick people from all aspects of your life (home, family, friends, activities, etc.).

______________	______________	______________
______________	______________	______________
______________	______________	______________
______________	______________	______________
______________	______________	______________
______________	______________	______________
______________	______________	______________
______________	______________	______________
______________	______________	______________

NOW, ASK YOURSELF: Is this person full of gratitude most of the time, or does this person have a Baditude? Choose the column that you think matches each person's attitude. Then, write a short reason to explain your choice.

Basement Attitudes	Balcony Attitudes

What's in It for Me? -- ACTIVITY #1

Step It UP!

INTRODUCTION

Imagine yourself looking up at a 10-foot staircase. On the top step is something that you really, really want to become or accomplish... you know, your dream for yourself! If you could, you would take one humongous step up to the top so you could have what you want right now... but that is physically impossible, and impossible in a lot of other ways too!

Materials Needed

- "Brainstorming" worksheet
- "Build the Staircase" worksheet
- Pencil or pen
- Colored pencils or markers
- Internet

Objectives

- Students will better understand that there are many steps involved when attempting to achieve a long-term goal. The greater the goal, the more involved the steps along the way become.
- Students will realize that all the "Need To's" in life are practice for the big things ahead.

Teacher Instructions

1. As a class, brainstorm a list of occupations/careers that interest your students.
2. Pass out the "Brainstorming" worksheets to the class.
3. Have each student select their dream profession, and write it on the "Brainstorming" worksheet.
4. Instruct students to:
   * Research online the selected profession, and all that it takes to get there.
   * Use the worksheet to organize your plan on what to do now, what to do next, etc., to achieve your goal.
   * Use your "Brainstorming" sheet to list the things from now to later that you need to do to achieve your goal.

5. Once the class has completed the "Brainstorming" worksheet, pass out the "Build the Staircase" worksheet to the class.
6. Instruct students to:
   * Print off or draw a picture of their dream job and glue it to the top of the staircase.
   * Write the steps (1 to 10) from the "Brainstorming" worksheet in chronological order on the steps from bottom (now) to top (later) on the "Build the Staircase" worksheet.
7. Allow students to present their finished staircases to the class, explaining each step.
8. Display for all to enjoy.

 Name ____________________

Brainstorming: Part 1

DIRECTIONS: Think about your dream job! Use the space below to write down all the things that might help you get that job.

What is my dream job?

What is needed to earn that job? ____________________

____

____

____

____

EDUCATION	EXPERIENCE

LOCATION

OTHER

Physical requirements?

Emotional requirements?

Cost requirements (money, time, etc.)?

Age requirements?

What steps are needed? ______________________________

____

____

____

____

____

____

____

Name ________________________

Build the Staircase: Part 2

DIRECTIONS: Step into your dream job! Draw or glue a picture that shows your dream job. Then, starting at the bottom of the staircase, write the steps you need to take to reach that job.

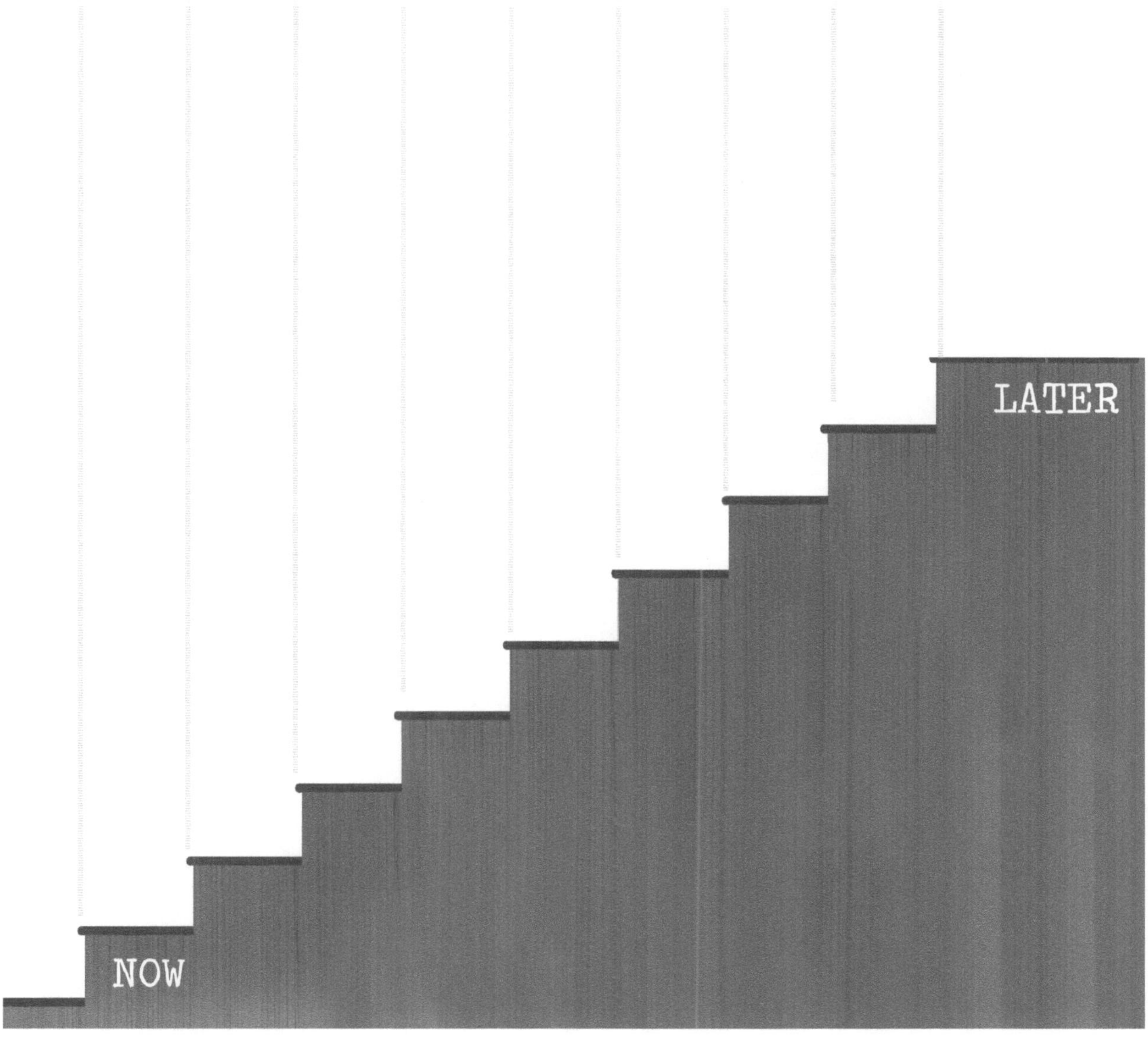

What's in It for Me? -- ACTIVITY #2

Who Inspires You?

INTRODUCTION

Who is the person who inspires you the most? A person who inspires has the ability to encourage you to feel something or do something that is creative. Sometimes, we know the people who inspire us very well. Some people never meet the person who inspires them the most – they inspire from afar through their actions.

Objectives

- Students will explain what it means to inspire someone.
- Students will identify who inspires them and explain why and how.

Materials Needed

- "Who Inspires You?" worksheet
- Construction paper
- Markers or colored pencils

Teacher Instructions

1. Pass out the "Who Inspires You?" worksheet to the class.
2. Instruct students to:
   * Fill out their worksheet.
   * Make a thank you card for the person who inspires them!
3. Display the card on the bulletin board for all to enjoy and then send each card to the inspiring individual.

 Name ______________________

Who Inspires You?

DIRECTIONS: Answer the questions below. Create a thank you card for the person who inspires you!

1. Who inspires you the most? Why? ______________________

____

____

____

2. Have you ever met this person? ______________________

____

3. List 5 things you have learned from the person who inspires you.

    1. ______________________
    2. ______________________
    3. ______________________
    4. ______________________
    5. ______________________

4. If you could talk to that person right now, what would you say? What questions would you ask that person? ______________________

____

____

____

5. How (in what ways) has this person made you better? ______________________

____

____

____

What's in It for Me? -- ACTIVITY #3

Switching NEED TOs into I DID ITs!

INTRODUCTION

Being told what we NEED TO do all of the time is like taking orders. A better option is thinking about what we GET TO do. A GET TO is an opportunity! A NEED TO is similar to a HAVE TO – which feels like an order. GET TOs are easier to get done! Then they can turn into I DID ITs!!!

Materials Needed

- *What's in It for Me?* storybook (optional)
- Pen or pencil
- "I DID IT!" worksheet

Objective

Students will learn to look at orders as opportunities.

Teacher Instructions

1. (Optional) Read *What's in It for Me?*, by Julia Cook, to the class.
2. As a group, brainstorm ideas for personal rewards (take a mental vacation, 10 minutes of free time, a walk around the school, 10 minutes of doing "nothing," etc.). List all personal rewards on the board for all to see.
3. Pass out the "I DID IT!" worksheet at the beginning of the day and have students list throughout the day what they need to do.
4. Have them rephrase each "NEED TO" into a "GET TO" and write it on the sheet.
5. Instruct students to check off every "I DID IT" as they get them done.
6. Choose a celebration reward and have students write it in the blank.
7. CELEBRATE your success!!!

Name ______________________________

I DID IT!

DIRECTIONS: Fill in the chart below. Once you complete the "NEED TOs/GET TOs," you can check the "I Did It!" box.

NEED TOs	GET TOs	I DID IT!
		☐
		☐
		☐
		☐
		☐
		☐
		☐

NEED TO  I DID IT

My "NEED TOs" are now "GET TOs"
I've checked off each one.
I'm going to celebrate!
I DID ITs are FUN!

I'm going to reward myself with...

____.

What's in It for Me? -- ACTIVITY #4

Why Does Noodle Need to?

INTRODUCTION

When a person sees the reason behind a **NEED TO**, it becomes much easier to convert that **NEED TO** into **GET TO!**

Objective

- Students will better recognize why **NEED TOs** are important.

Materials Needed

- *What's in It for Me?* storybook
- Metal clothes hanger for each student
- 3"x5" index cards
- Paper hole punch
- Yarn or string
- Colored pencils or markers

Teacher Instructions

1. Read *What's in it for me?,* by Julia Cook, and have students write 5 or 6 of the **NEED TOs** that Noodle is given on separate cards – one idea per card (pull the weeds, put laundry away, etc.).
2. Create one more card with a **NEED TO** that you've been given in your own life (study your spelling words, push in your chair, feed the dog, etc.).
3. On the back of each card, draw a picture of what might happen if the **"NEED TO"** doesn't get done.
4. Have students punch a hole in each of their cards, then cut a piece of string or yarn and thread it through the hole. Instruct them to tie each card to their hanger to create a mobile, as shown in the illustration.
5. Have students attach their unique **"NEED TO"** card to the rest of the cards, as shown in the illustration.

6. Allow each child to share their unique **"NEED TO"** card and mobile with the class.
7. Display for all to enjoy!

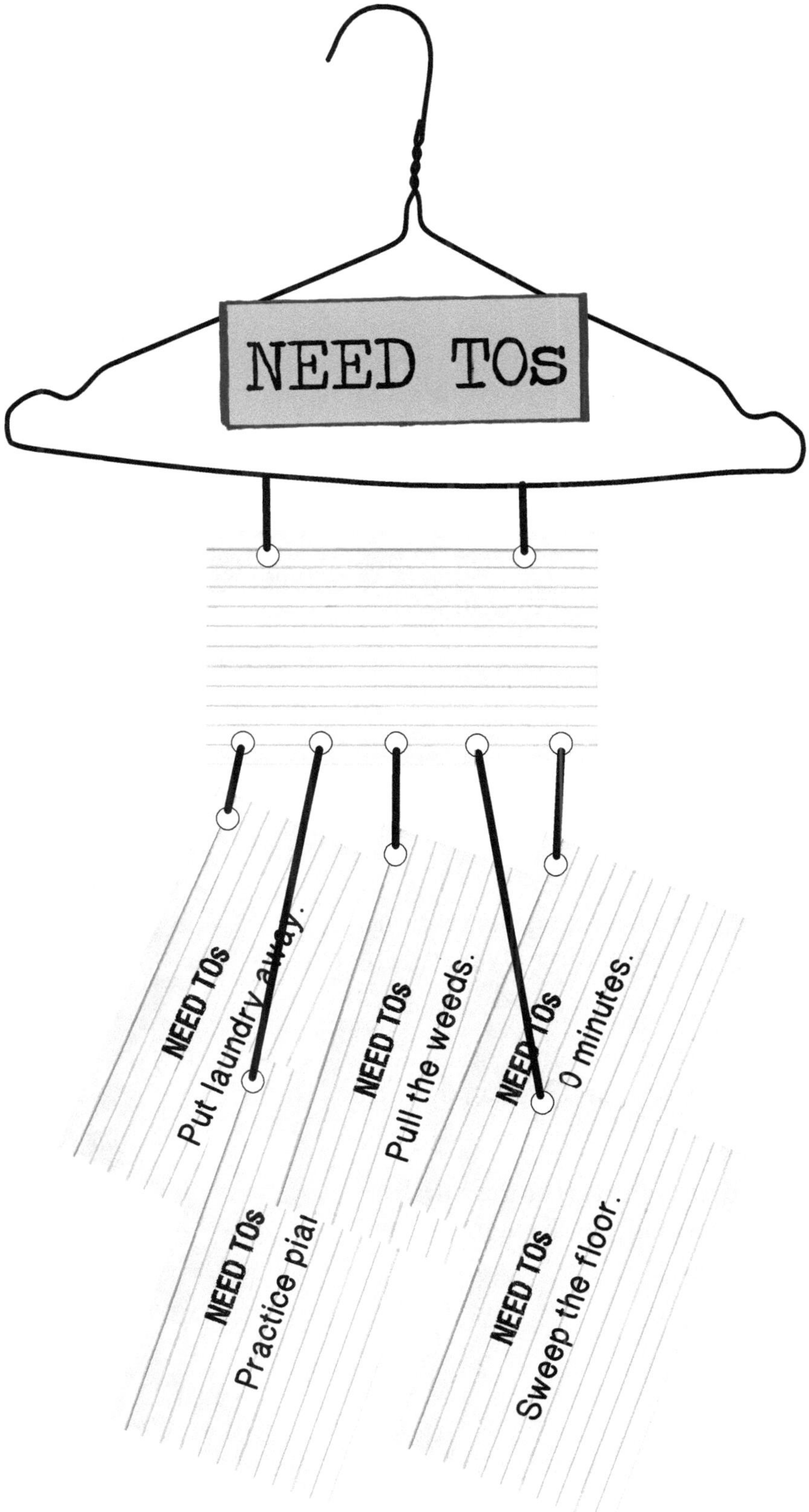

But It's Not My Fault -- ACTIVITY #1

My Responsibility Kit

INTRODUCTION

Taking responsibility for your own actions is a learned behavior that is VITAL to character development. Everyone makes mistakes, and mistakes are a good thing because every mistake made offers you a learning opportunity. If you blame other people for your mistakes, you give away that opportunity. Here is a little kit that can help you remember to be responsible and stay responsible.

Objective

Students will use the items in this kit to create visual reminders to be and stay responsible.

Materials Needed (one of each, per student)

- "My Responsibility Tool Kit" handout
- Small plastic Ziploc bag – quart or sandwich size
- Band aids
- Paper clips
- Cotton balls
- Erasers
- Buttons
- Small pieces of golden thread
- Mints
- Rubber band
- Life saver
- Price tags

Teacher Instructions

1. Place items in piles and have students take one of each item from the piles, carefully placing them in their Ziploc bags.
2. Distribute the "My Responsibility Tool Kit" handout. Together, review and explain the purpose of each item.
3. Allow students to keep the kits at their desks as a reminder of the importance of being responsible.

My Responsibility Tool Kit

Button	To remind me to button my lips and think about my own actions before blaming others.
Band Aid	To help heal hurt feelings on the inside and the out.
Eraser	To remind me that everyone makes mistakes – and that's okay! Mistakes help me learn and grow.
Mint	Being and acting responsible is worth a mint!
Golden thread	To remind me to use the "Golden Rule" – Treat others the way I would like to be treated.
Paper clip	To help me hold everything together.
Rubber band	To remind me NOT to stretch the truth and stay flexible when things get tough.
Cotton ball	To remind me that being irresponsible can snowball out of control very quickly.
Life Saver	To remind me that being responsible can save my life.
Price tag	To remind me that being responsible is worth a lot – even more than money.

But It's Not My Fault -- ACTIVITY #2

I Had a Hand in That!

INTRODUCTION

Everyone makes mistakes. When you own a mistake, you can learn from the experience. One of the more difficult things to do in life is to admit it when you do something wrong. Great people make great mistakes... and then they learn. If you blame someone else for a mistake that you made, you give away that opportunity to learn.

Objective

Students will better understand how owning their mistakes can help them grow.

Materials Needed

- White or light-colored construction paper
- Pencil
- Scissors
- Fine line marker
- Colored pencil or crayon

Teacher Instructions

1. Have students trace their handprint and cut it out.
2. Ask students to fill in the palm print with words or drawings using the following guide:

   Palm: Your name (optional).
   Thumb: A mistake that you made.
   Index Finger: What was something negative that happened as a result of your mistake?
   Long Finger: What did you do/or what are you going to do in the future to own it?
   Ring Finger: What happened when you took responsibility for your action?
   Pinkie: What did you learn from making that mistake?

   TEACHER NOTE: You may want to coach students before the activity. Because their handprints will be displayed, encourage them to choose a mistake that won't cause them embarrassment or make their classmates uncomfortable.

3. Have students share their handprint with others and then display them on a bulletin board that has a slogan at the top: "Great people make great mistakes," "I had a hand in that," "Mistakes can help me grow," or "Don't be a BLAMER."

But It's Not My Fault -- ACTIVITY #3

Don't Blame ME!

INTRODUCTION

Sometimes a great way to learn about the effects of blaming others is to reflect upon a time when somebody blamed you for something you didn't do. Empathy is KEY in developing personal responsibility for your actions.

Objectives

- Students will gain empathy for others.
- Students will reduce their tendencies toward blaming others.
- Students will improve their active listening and repeating skills.
- Students will increase their levels of responsibility for self.

Materials Needed

- *But It's Not My Fault* storybook (optional)
- "Don't Blame Me" worksheet
- Pencil or pen

Teacher Instructions

1. (Optional) Read *But It's Not My Fault,* by Julia Cook, to the class and discuss times when and why Noodle blamed others.
2. Pass out the "Don't Blame Me" worksheets to the class.
3. Have students complete their worksheets.
4. Sort students into groups of 3-4, then have them discuss with their groups what they wrote on their sheets.
5. Instruct students to:
   * Have the person to the right of you stand up and explain what you were blamed for, how you felt, why you think the person blamed you, what you did about it, and how this experience has changed you.

Name ____________________________

Don't Blame ME!

DIRECTIONS: Answer the questions below. Be prepared to have your answers shared in class.

1. Describe a time when you were blamed for something that you did not do. ____________

____

____

____

2. How did that make you feel? ______________________________

____

____

____

3. Why do you think the person blamed you? ______________________

____

____

____

4. What did you do about it? ______________________________

____

____

____

5. Did this experience change you in any way? If so, how?

____

____

____

____

____

But It's Not My Fault -- ACTIVITY #4

My MOTTO!

INTRODUCTION

Being responsible is a choice that starts with you! Are you making good decisions both with your mind and your body? There is only one you! How can you become the best "YOU" that you can be? What do you see when you look in the mirror? Do you do the right thing even when no one is looking?

Materials Needed

- Scratch paper
- Markers or colored pencils
- Poster board (8"x10")

Summary

- Students will design a logo and write a motto that shows who they are and who they want to become.

Teacher Instructions

1. Pass out scratch paper to each student.
2. Ask students to create their own personal motto or logo that represents how they can become their best self.
3. Instruct students to:
   * Do an online search and take note of famous mottos and logos as a springboard for ideas.
   * Write down 5 adjectives and 5 adverbs that best describe you and how you are responsible.
   * Using the information you came up with, work in groups of 3-4 and brainstorm ideas for your motto and logo. Keep in mind, your logo should relate somehow to being a responsible person.
   * Practice drawing your logo and writing your motto on the scratch paper.
   * Create your logo and motto on the poster board, explain the meaning, and display for all to enjoy.

The PROcrastinator -- ACTIVITY #1

Rocks, Pebbles, and Sand

INTRODUCTION

Life is full of things we have to do, things we need to do, and things we want to do. Since time is a limited commodity, we have to be strategic in planning out our time so that we can get everything done and still have enough time left over to have fun and enjoy life.

Objective

Students will analyze and explain how owning their mistakes can help them grow.

Materials Needed (Quantities needed must be pre-measured and determined in advance depending on the size of the bowls used. See steps 4 and 5 to determine quantities.)

- 2 identical clear glass bowls or containers
- 2 piles of large rocks
- 2 piles of small pebbles
- 2 equal amounts of sand
- Marker board or chalk board
- Markers or chalk

Teacher Instructions

1. As a class, brainstorm things in life that we have to do, things in life that we need to do, and things in life that we want to do. (Examples may include: get enough sleep, eat, exercise, play video games, complete homework and assignments, go to team practices, play outside, study for tests, practice musical instruments, etc.)
2. Hold up the empty bowl and explain that what it can hold represents how much time we have.
3. Introduce the large rocks as things in life that we have to do, the pebbles as things that we need to do or should do, and the sand as things that we want to do.
4. In the first bowl, place the large rocks symbolizing the things we have to do. Then follow with pebbles symbolizing the things

we need to do, and end by pouring in the sand (things we want to do). Notice how everything fits in the bowl perfectly.

5. In the second bowl, place the sand in first – doing what we want to do, then follow with the pebbles – what we should do or need to do, and finish by adding in the big rocks – things we have to do. Point out how the rocks, pebbles, and sand don't fit inside the bowl, as there is not enough room.
6. Summarize by explaining that if we do the things we have to do and should do first, we can usually fit in what we want to do. But if we reverse this, we can rarely get done what needs to get done.

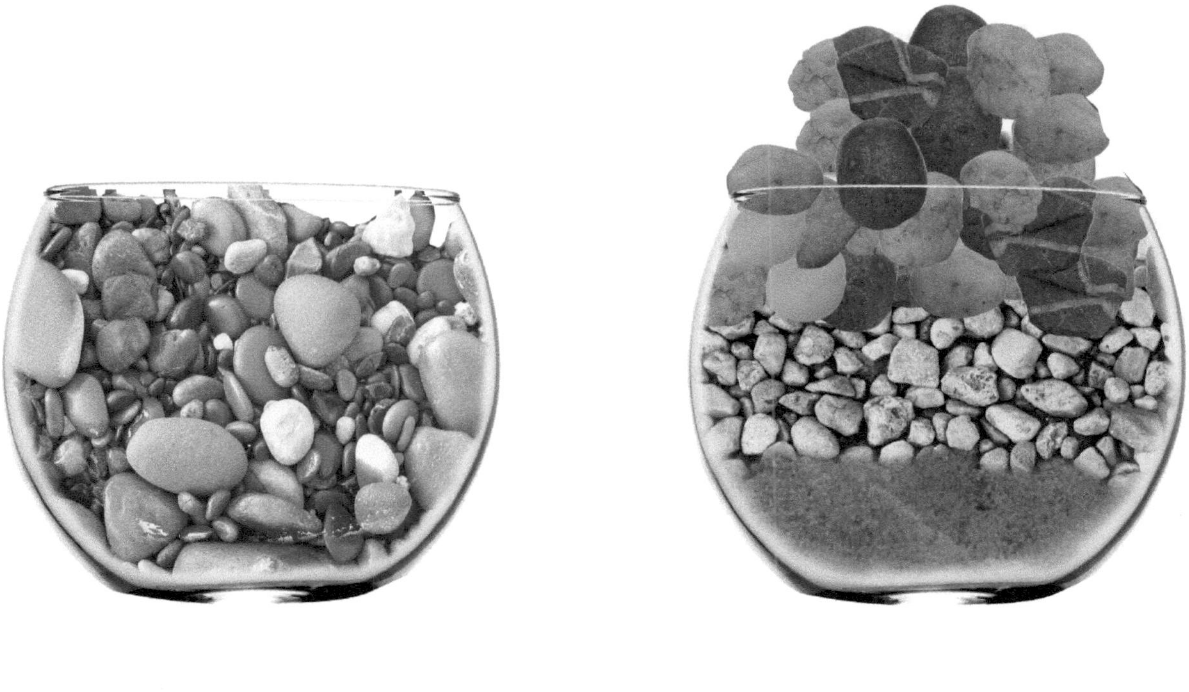

The PROcrastinator -- ACTIVITY #2

Project Tsunami Prevention!

INTRODUCTION

When a project with many small parts is assigned, students often have a difficult time planning out what to do and when. This sometimes leads to procrastination. When left to the last minute, successful completion of the project changes from a wave into a tsunami. Planning and prioritizing are two of the most difficult executive function skills for people to master.

Planning effectively is the thinking skill that helps an individual develop strategies to accomplish goals. It allows a person to think about completing a task before it is started. Life is all about making choices and prioritizing effectively helps a person make the best choices possible. Time is a limited commodity and to get the most out of your time, and accomplish all that you need to do, you have to be able to plan and prioritize both on a long- and short-term basis.

Objective

Students will practice how to be more successful at planning and making priorities.

Materials Needed

- *The PROcrastinator* storybook (optional)
- A large project or assignment involving many parts
- "Tsunami Prevention Planning" worksheet
- Pen or pencil
- Various project supplies

Teacher Instructions

1. (Optional) Read *The PROcrastinator,* by Julia Cook, to the class.
2. Explain to students that they will be using a planning worksheet to help them prioritize and plan a major project.
3. Pass out the "Tsunami Prevention Planning" worksheets to students.
4. Instruct students to fill out the planning sheet prior to starting on the project, and use it until the project is completed.

 Name ______________________________

Tsunami Prevention Planning Sheet

NAME OF PROJECT/ASSIGNMENT: ______________________________

DUE DATE: ______________________________

NAME(S):______________________________

1. Think about your overall plan. What is your ultimate goal?

2. Make a list of everything that needs to be done to accomplish your goal, when and who will do it, and what supplies are needed.

SUPPLIES	NEEDS TO BE DONE	WHEN/WHO
1.	1.	1.
2.	2.	2.
3.	3.	3.
4.	4.	4.
5.	5.	5.

3. Rank the items on your list in order of importance. Think about what is urgent. What needs to be done NOW, and what can be done later?

4. Determine the differences between your needs and your wants.

5. Decide what things on your list are BIG things (must do's to make this assignment happen) and what things are small things (may seem very important to you now, but may not be quite as important to you a few weeks or months from now).

6. Think about the consequences involved if you don't get the stuff on your list done.

7. Anticipate things that might go wrong and make a plan for what to do if that happens.

8. If you make a mistake while completing your project, make note of it, learn from it, and do your best not to make that same mistake again in the future.

*** *When your project is completed, use this space to write a short paragraph.* ***

Was using this sheet helpful to you? Why or why not? ______________________________

____

____

____

____

The PROcrastinator -- ACTIVITY #3

Sundae Fun Day!

INTRODUCTION

Sometimes putting stuff off can lead to a not-so-great situation.

Objective

Students will define and recognize what procrastination looks like.

Materials Needed

- One freshly made large (over filling the dish) sundae with lots of toppings (whipped cream, caramel, chocolate, etc.)

Teacher Instructions

1. Walk into your classroom with a freshly made sundae and explain how excited you are to eat it and how great you think it will taste. Place the sundae in your room so it can be viewed by all.
2. Proceed to teach away, and as the ice cream on the sundae starts to melt and make a mess, students will likely ask, "Aren't you going to eat your ice cream?" "When are you going to eat that sundae?"
3. Answer the students, "Oh yes, as soon as I have a minute. I'm starving. Can't wait to eat it...."
4. When the sundae is totally melted, act sad and relate how putting something off too long might result in a "runny sundae mess."
5. (Bring some goodies to share with the class.)

The PROcrastinator -- ACTIVITY #4

Procrastination Pizza

INTRODUCTION

Pacing yourself during a big project can be a lot more effective than trying to do the whole project all at once.

Objective

Students will practice time management while completing a large project with many parts.

Materials Needed

- Cardboard circle 16" in diameter (Corrugated cardboard works best, but any cardboard will work.)
- Assignment or project with many parts
- Red felt or red construction paper
- Colored paper pizza toppings – green peppers made out of green paper; pepperoni made out of red with white spots, etc.
- Markers or crayons
- Pieces of white cut-up yarn to represent cheese
- Scissors
- Paper
- Ruler
- Pencil

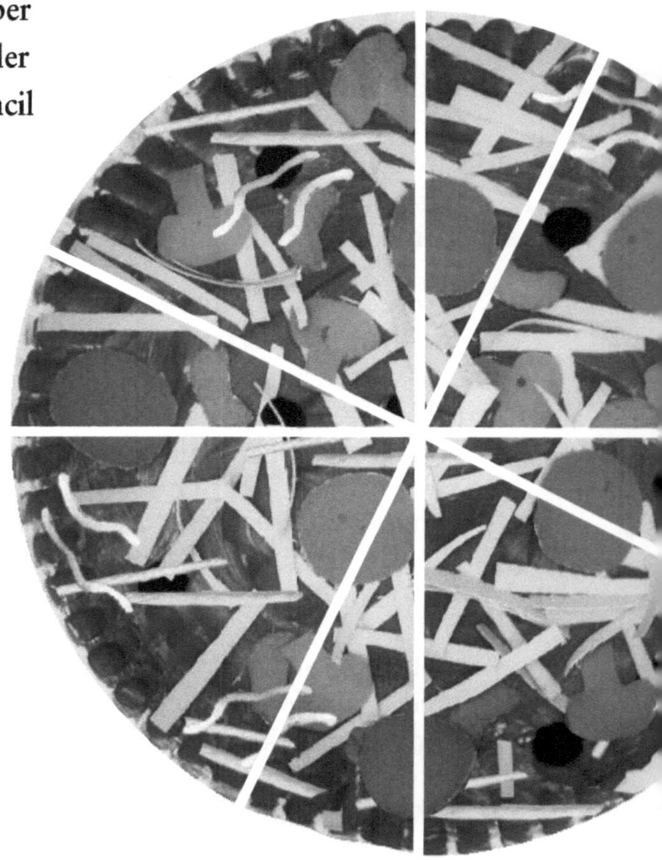

Teacher Instructions

1. Assign a project with many parts needed to fit together for completion (research project, science fair project, etc.).
2. Have students make a list of everything they need to do to complete the project and estimate how much time each part or step will take.
3. Add up the individual times and explain that the whole pizza represents the total amount of time.
4. Have students make a pizza out of the cardboard. Divide it into slices that show how much time each part of the assignment will take. Bigger slices = more time.
5. As soon as each project part is completed, let students decorate that corresponding piece of pizza with the topping of their choice.
6. When the pizza is fully decorated, the project should be completed.
7. Explain that eating one or two slices of pizza at a time is much easier than eating the whole pizza at once. Then show how this is like working on a big project: if you do a little at a time, it's easier than waiting and trying to do everything at once.

Cheaters Never Prosper -- ACTIVITY #1

Why Did You Do It?

INTRODUCTION

People cheat for numerous reasons, but that doesn't ever make it right. Finding out more about the reasons behind cheating and its effects on people can help kids better understand why in the long run – "Cheaters Never Prosper!"

Objectives

- Students will identify reasons why some people cheat.
- Students will examine the consequences of cheating.
- Students will assess their own feelings about cheating.

Materials Needed

- *Cheaters Never Prosper* storybook (optional)
- 10 copies, per student, of the "Why Did You Do It?" interview sheet
- 1 copy, per student, of the "Why Did You Do It?" summary sheet
- Pen or pencil
- 1 copy, per student, of the summary sheet

Teacher Instructions

1. (Optional) Read *Cheaters Never Prosper,* by Julia Cook, to the class and discuss Noodle's cheating.
2. Pass out 10 copies of the "Why Did You Do It?" interview sheets, and one copy of the summary sheet to each student.
3. Explain to students that they will interview 10 people of various ages, interests, and backgrounds.
4. Have students summarize the data on the summary sheet.

Cheaters Never Prosper -- ACTIVITY #1 Name of Person Interviewed: ______________________

Why Did You Do It? Interview Sheet

DIRECTIONS: Ask the questions below, then record the person's answers.

1. Think of a time in your life when you cheated (in school, at sports, in a game, at work, etc.).

2. What was happening that made you feel like you had to cheat?

3. How were you feeling when you decided to do that?

4. Was the outcome good or bad?

5. Looking back, how do you feel about it now?

Cheaters Never Prosper -- ACTIVITY #1 Name of Person Interviewed: ______________________

Why Did You Do It? Interview Sheet

DIRECTIONS: Ask the questions below, then record the person's answers.

1. Think of a time in your life when you cheated (in school, at sports, in a game, at work, etc.).

2. What was happening that made you feel like you had to cheat?

3. How were you feeling when you decided to do that?

4. Was the outcome good or bad?

5. Looking back, how do you feel about it now?

 Name ______________________

Why Did You Do It? Summary Sheet

DIRECTIONS: Answer the questions below based on your interview.

1. Based on your interviews, why do you think people cheat? ______________________

2. How do you feel about cheating now? ______________________

3. What was one thing that you learned by doing the interviews? ______________________

4. Has this experience changed you in any way? If yes, how?

Cheaters Never Prosper -- ACTIVITY #2

Cheating Stars

INTRODUCTION

Celebrities and sports heroes are often looked up to by many. When someone famous cheats and gets caught, we often feel like someone took something valuable away from us – our admiration.

Objective

Students will recognize how cheating can affect others.

Materials Needed

- *Cheaters Never Prosper* storybook (optional)
- Internet
- "Cheating Stars" worksheet
- Pencil or pen

Teacher Instructions

1. (Optional) Read *Cheaters Never Prosper,* by Julia Cook, to the class and discuss Noodle's cheating.
2. Pass out the "Cheating Stars" worksheet to students.
3. Instruct students to:
   - Research a celebrity or sports hero who has been caught cheating.
   - Fill out their worksheet.
   - Discuss their findings in small groups, then with the class.

 Name ____________________

Cheating Stars

DIRECTIONS: Answer the questions below.

1. Who is your cheating star? ____________________

2. How did they cheat? ____________________
____
____

3. Why do you think they cheated? ____________________
____
____

4. What could that person have done differently? ____________________
____
____

5. What is your opinion of that person now? ____________________
____
____

6. Should consequences for cheating be more severe for famous people? Why or why not? ____________________
____
____

7. What did you learn from doing this activity? ____________________
____
____

Cheaters Never Prosper -- ACTIVITY #3

Cheater Detours!

INTRODUCTION

People cheat for numerous reasons. If we can learn useful strategies to counteract the feelings associated with the need to cheat, we can decrease the occurrence!

Objective

Students will identify useful strategies that can help combat the occurrence of cheating.

Materials Needed

- "What Can You Do to Prevent Cheating" worksheet
- Pencil or pen
- White board or chalk board
- Dry erase markers or chalk
- Poster board or bulletin board paper
- Markers

Teacher Instructions

1. Pass out the "What Can You Do to Prevent Cheating?" worksheet and have students work on it independently.
2. Using the letters in the title *Cheaters Never Prosper*, come up with a cheating-prevention strategy or tip for each letter. Write your tip next to the letter.

For example:

C – **CLEAR** your head of everything except what you need to remember for the test.

H – Ask for **HELP** when you don't understand something.

3. Allow students to work independently for 15-20 minutes.

   NOTE: By allowing individual time, the quiet/reserved thinkers will have a chance to create and be able to have something to contribute to the group as opposed to getting talked over.

4. Divide the class into groups of 3-4 and have them discuss and consolidate their ideas on one sheet.

5. Have each group share their ideas. Then, work together as a class to make one list of strategies.

6. Write out the strategies onto bulletin board paper or poster board and display for all to see.

7. Reinforce/review these strategies often.

NOTE

Keep in mind that when kids come up with the strategies, they are much more likely to use them!

 Name ______________________

What Can You Do to Prevent Cheating?

DIRECTIONS: For each letter in the title *Cheaters Never Prosper,* think of a strategy to help prevent cheating. Write your strategy next to the letter.

C ______________________
H ______________________
E ______________________
A ______________________
T ______________________
E ______________________
R ______________________
S ______________________

N ______________________
E ______________________
V ______________________
E ______________________
R ______________________

P ______________________
R ______________________
O ______________________
S ______________________
P ______________________
E ______________________
R ______________________

Cheaters Never Prosper -- ACTIVITY #4

Just 5 Words and 1 Phrase

INTRODUCTION

Knowing how our actions affect others can make us think twice about the decisions we make.

Objective

Students will recognize and explain how cheating affects others.

Materials Needed

- "How Do You Feel?" handout pages of 10 cards each (2 per student)
- Colored pencils or markers
- Large construction paper
- Pen or pencil
- Graph paper
- Scratch paper

Teacher Instructions

1. Distribute the "How Do You Feel?" handout to each student.
2. Have students ask 20 different people to give them 5 words that describe how they feel when someone cheats. Then, have each person sum up their opinion in one sentence or phrase. At least half of the people interviewed should be from outside school. (You may do 10 interviews instead of 20 for younger students.)
3. Instruct students to:
   * Ask each person you interview to sum up their opinion about cheating in a short sentence or phrase. For example: "You cannot cheat yourself" or "Cheaters never prosper!"
   * Write that sentence in the small space at the bottom of the cards.
   * Tally the single words and make a graph indicating how many of each word are listed. For example: 7 people said mad; 14 people said sad, etc.

* Graph your results of who said what.
* From all the sentences or phrases you collected, choose your favorite. Or, if you have a better idea, create your own!
* Glue your graph to the construction paper. Underneath it, write your favorite phrase about how cheating makes others (and/or you) feel.
* Explain your graph and your chosen phrase to the class. Then share one thing you learned from this activity.

TEACHER NOTE

Make copies of the "How Do You Feel?" handout (2 per student). Instruct students to ask 20 different people to tell them 5 words describing how they feel when someone cheats. Then, have each person interviewed sum up their opinion in a sentence or phrase.

How Do You Feel?

That Rule Doesn't Apply To Me! -- ACTIVITY #1

Gum Drop - Drop

INTRODUCTION

When people don't follow the rules or "adjust" rules to make them fit better, it can be very frustrating to others.

Materials Needed

- Cotton swabs (2 for each team of 3-4 students)
- Gumdrops (spice drops) 3 for each child
- Empty, clean 20 oz soda bottle with lid removed (1 per team)
- Team reward – free assignment pass, candy, free time, etc.

Objectives

- Students will identify feelings associated with noncompliance and how these feelings affect others.
- Students will recognize why rules are important, and what could happen if we didn't have rules.

Teacher Instructions

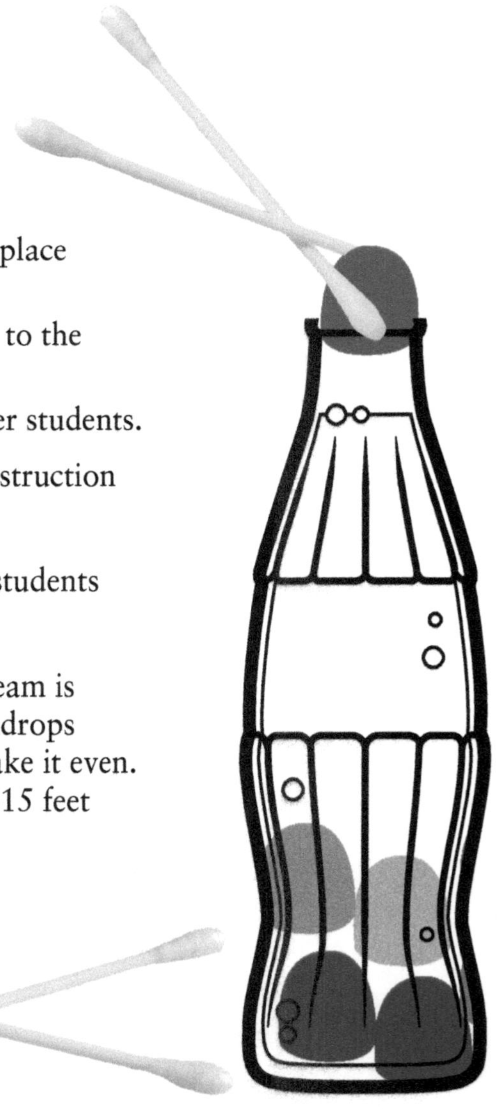

1. Before starting the activity, select 3-4 students and privately explain the following:
   * They should hold the cotton swabs in one hand.
   * They should pick up the gumdrops by hand and place them into the 20 oz bottle.
   * This is different from what you will demonstrate to the rest of the class.
   * Ask them not to share this information with other students.

   Choose students who are comfortable keeping this instruction confidential.

2. Divide the class into groups of 3-4 (making sure the students chosen above are all in the same group).

3. Set up game courses in your classroom, where each team is given two cotton swabs and an equal number of gumdrops (2-3 each). Some students will need to go twice to make it even. Place gumdrops and cotton swabs approximately 10-15 feet from each empty bottle.

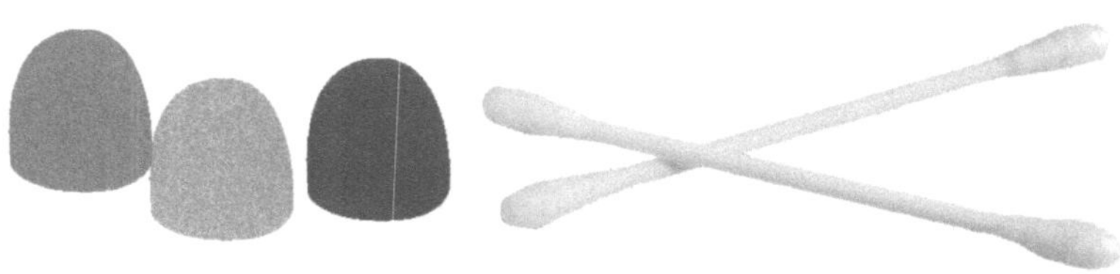

4. Explain and demonstrate the following:
   * This activity is a relay. Each member of your team takes a turn.
   * While holding the cotton swabs, grab the gum drop, carry it to the bottle, and drop it in.

     NOTE: (Do not say this aloud – just show it):
     - Hold one cotton swab in each hand.
     - Use the swabs to squeeze and hold the gumdrop.
     - Drop the gumdrop into the bottle without touching it with your fingers.
   * Everyone will go twice and some may need to go three times to make it even. The first team that gets all of the gumdrops into the bottle wins.
5. Run the relay. Naturally, the team carrying the gumdrops by hand will win. Students will notice the rule-breaking and complain. At that point, one member of the winning team should respond:
   * "You said, 'While holding the cotton swabs, grab the gumdrop, carry it to the bottle, and drop it in.' That's exactly what we did!"
6. Lead a class discussion about how people feel when others don't follow the rules, why we have to have rules, and why rules are so important.
7. Reveal to the groups that you instructed the winning team to play differently in order to win, so there are no hard feelings.
8. Replay the relay. This time, everyone follows the same rules.

That Rule Doesn't Apply To Me! -- ACTIVITY #2

Connect-the-Dots!

INTRODUCTION

Sometimes, when we don't follow the rules—or don't fully understand them—the outcome isn't as good as it could be.

Objective

Students will examine why knowing what the rules are and following them correctly is important.

Materials Needed

- "Numbered Connect-the-Dots" worksheet
- "You Decide Connect-the-Dots" worksheet
- One, per student, of each type of connect-the-dot pages (A and B)
- Pencil
- Crayons or markers

Teacher Instructions

1. Pass out the "You Decide Connect-the-Dots" worksheet. Have students complete the worksheet and then share their answers with the group.
2. Pass out the "Numbered Connect-the-Dots" worksheet and have students complete it.
3. Have students compare the two papers.
4. Discuss why following rules can make a big difference when it comes to outcomes.
5. Instruct students to color in their "Numbered Connect-the Dots" worksheet.

Name ______________________________

A Numbered Connect-the-Dots

DIRECTIONS: Connect the dots to create a recognizable picture of Noodle. Begin at the point labeled "Start here."

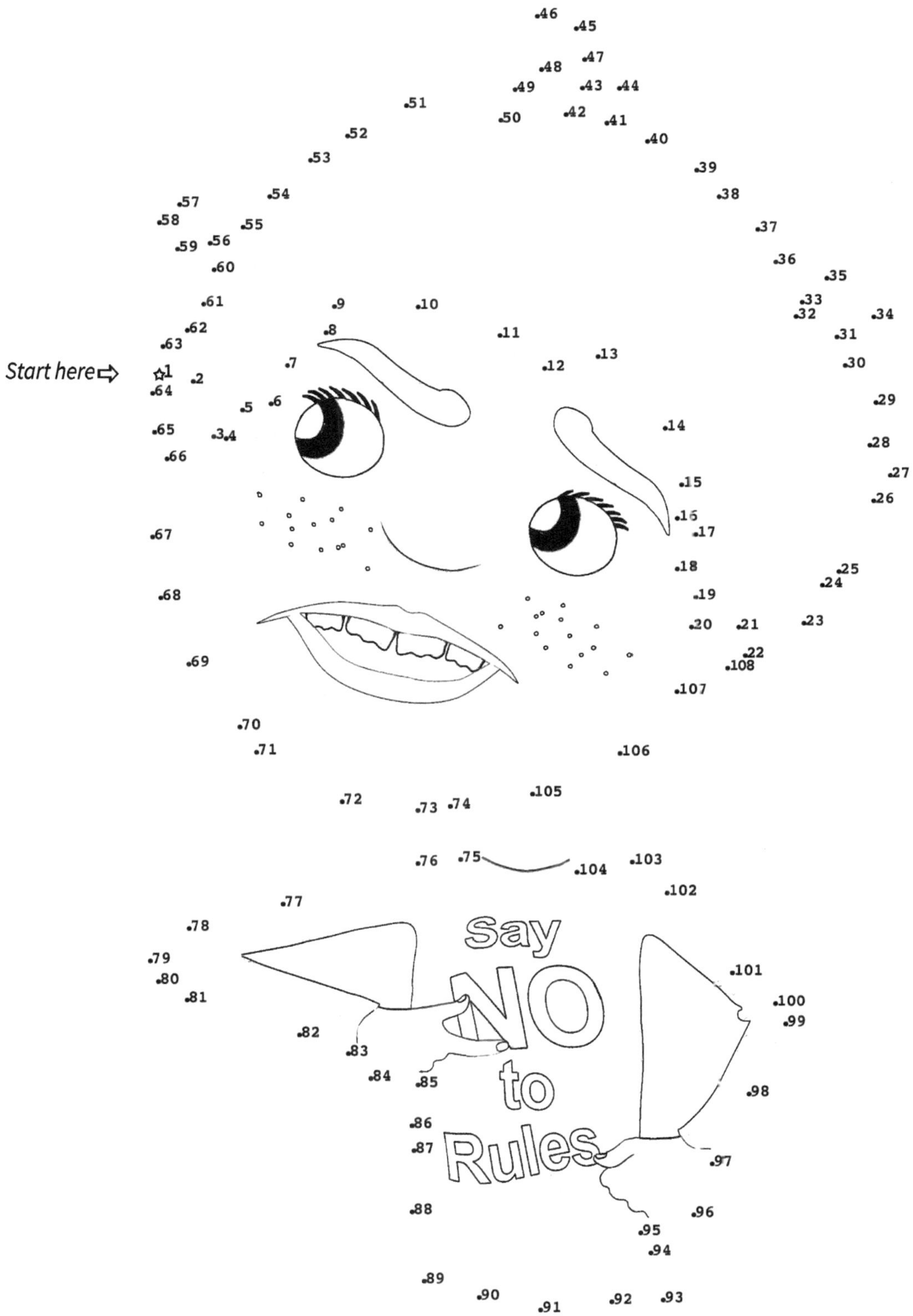

B You Decide Connect-the-Dots

DIRECTIONS: Connect the dots to create a recognizable picture of Noodle.

That Rule Doesn't Apply To Me! -- ACTIVITY #3

Rules in My Name!

INTRODUCTION Can you use the letters in your name to think up rules that are important for all to follow?

Objective

Students will correctly use their first names during the activity and explain how following rules affects fairness and outcomes.

Materials Needed

- *That Rule Doesn't Apply to Me* storybook (optional)
- Scratch Paper
- Dictionary
- Pencil
- Poster board
- Markers or colored pencils

Teacher Instructions

1. (Optional) Read *That Rule Doesn't Apply to Me,* by Julia Cook, to the class.
2. Pass out scratch paper to all students.
3. Instruct students to:
   * Write your first name at the top of the scratch paper.
   * Think of a rule that starts with each letter in your name and write it down. (For example: J = Jumping rope is only allowed outside.) If you can't think of anything, look up words in the dictionary that start with that letter until you get a good idea.
   * Transfer your information onto the poster using colorful markers or colored pencils. Share your poster with the rest of the class.
4. Pull from the student-generated rules to come up with your set of unique, kid-organic classroom rules.

That Rule Doesn't Apply To Me! -- ACTIVITY #4

Kids Rule!

INTRODUCTION

If students take an active part in creating their classroom rules, the rules become much more meaningful and easier to follow.

Objective

- Students will participate in a needs assessment and contribute ideas during a class discussion to help create classroom rules.
- Students will describe reasons why rules are needed and explain why following them is important during a class discussion.

Materials Needed

- *That Rule Doesn't Apply to Me* storybook (optional)
- Large poster board or piece of bulletin board paper
- Markers or crayons
- Pencils or Pens
- Marker board or chalk board (dry erase markers or chalk)
- "Kids Rule" worksheet

Teacher Instructions

1. (Optional) Read *That Rule Doesn't Apply to Me,* by Julia Cook, to the class.
2. Pass out the "Kids Rule" worksheets and have students complete them independently.
3. Divide the class into groups of 3-4. Have them discuss their worksheet answers and create an activity sheet that includes each group member's answers.
4. Have one member from each group share their answers with the class. Write each unique answer on the chalkboard (do not repeat duplicates).
5. Condense the list into 5 statements that summarize the answers as a whole.
6. As a class, create 5 classroom rules that represent those statements. This may involve voting and making compromises.
7. Have one student write the 5 classroom rules on a poster board or large bulletin board paper. Then, have each student sign their name under the rules to show they agree to follow them.
8. Display the classroom rule poster in a visible spot so everyone can see it.

 Name ______________________

Kids Rule

DIRECTIONS: Answer the questions below.

1. How would you like me to treat you in this class?

2. What things do teachers do that make learning harder or less enjoyable for you?

3. How would you like other students to treat you in this class?

4. What things do other students do that make learning harder or less enjoyable for you?

5. What is your favorite memory from school so far?

6. How did you feel during that moment? Why do you think you felt that way?

7. What is a school memory that was difficult or made you feel unhappy?

8. How did you feel during that moment? What made you feel that way?

9. Give an example of a great classroom rule.

10. Give an example of a terrible classroom rule.

11. If we could only have one classroom rule, what should it be?

Boys Town Press Books by Julia Cook

Responsible ME!

Kid-friendly titles to teach social skills

A book series that delivers a powerful message about accountability and honesty.

978-1-944882-09-9

978-1-944882-30-3

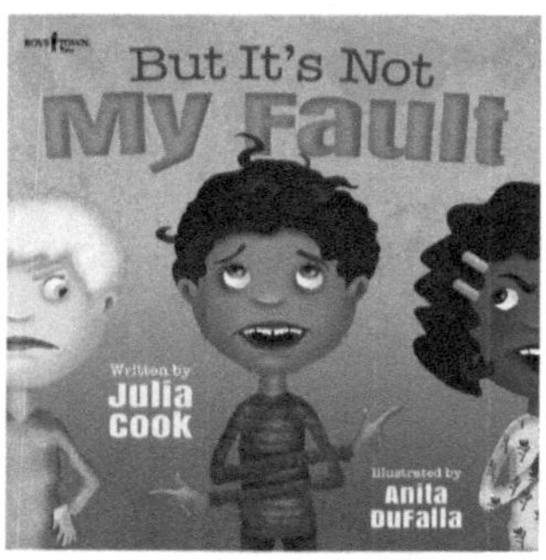

978-1-934490-80-8

978-1-934490-90-7

978-1-934490-98-3

978-1-944882-08-2

More Award-Winning Children's Book Series from Julia Cook

The LEADER I'll Be! · BEST ME I Can Be! · Socially Skilled Kids · Building RELATIONSHIPS · Awesome DAWSON · Best START · COMMUNICATE with Confidence

Every Donation *Makes a Difference*

More than 3.5 million children and families across the United States benefit from Boys Town's innovative programs each year. Our wide-ranging initiatives include youth care, healthcare and research, educational opportunities and parenting resources.

Help us write the next chapter by donating today. Because when you give children and families hope, you change their future.

BOYS TOWN. Saving Children Healing Families

boystown.org/donate

SCAN TO DONATE

BOYS TOWN® Press

For information on Boys Town and its Education Model, Common Sense Parenting®, and training programs:
LiftwithBoysTown.org | Parenting.org
training@boystown.org | 800-545-5771

For parenting and educational books and other resources:
BoysTownPress.org
btpress@boystown.org | 800-282-6657